Growing Up in
Wild Horse Canyon

KAREN AUTIO *Illustrated by* LORAINE KEMP

Reading makes you grow!
Karen Autio

Let your creativity take root!
Loraine Kemp

LIBRARY AND ARCHIVES CANADA CATALOGUING IN PUBLICATION

Autio, Karen, 1958–, author
   Growing up in Wild Horse Canyon / Karen Autio;
illustrated by Loraine Kemp.
Issued in print and electronic formats.
ISBN 978-1-77533-190-2 (hardcover).
ISBN 978-1-77533-192-6 (EPUB).
ISBN 978-1-77533-191-9 (PDF).

   1. Okanagan Valley (B.C.)—History—Juvenile literature.
I. Kemp, Loraine, illustrator II. Title.

FC3845.O4A98 2018   j971.1'5   C2018-903825-X
C2018-903826-8

Edited by Laura Peetoom
Copy edited by Dawn Loewen
Proofread by Audrey McClellan
Editorial advising by Jordan Coble
Cover and interior design by Frances Hunter
Maps by Paperglyphs

Published by
Crwth Press
#204 – 2320 Woodland Drive
Vancouver, BC V5N 3P2

orders@crwth.ca
www.crwth.ca

Printed and bound in Canada

Crwth Press is committed to environmentally
sustainable practices. This book is printed on
Forestry Stewardship Council (FSC) paper.

FSC
www.fsc.org

MIX
Paper from
responsible sources
FSC® C016245

Dedicated to the syilx people,

on whose lands this story unfolds,

in celebration of the beauty of creation

and history of place

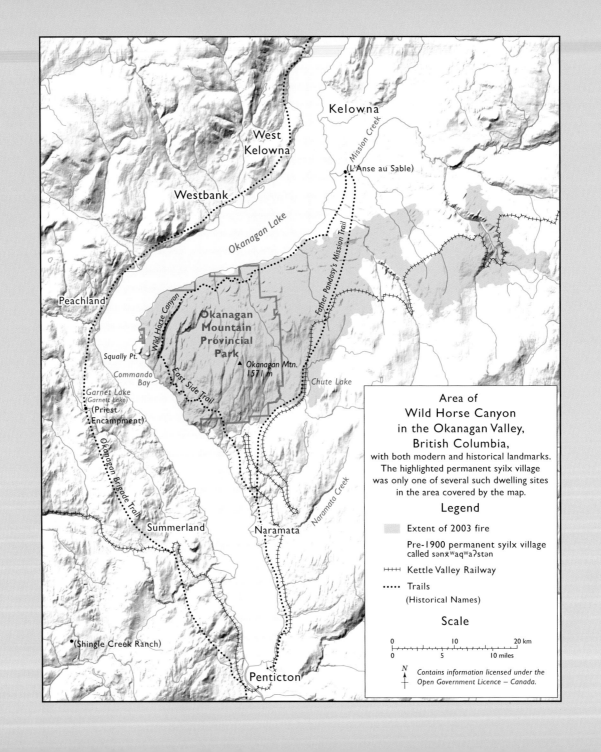

Kelowna

West
Kelowna

Westbank

Mission Creek

(L'Anse au Sable)

Okanagan Lake

Father Pandosy's Mission Trail

Peachland

Wild Horse Canyon

**Okanagan
Mountain
Provincial
Park**

Squally Pt.

East Side Trail

▲ Okanagan Mtn.
1571 m

Commando
Bay

Chute Lake

Garnet Lake
(Garnett Lake)
(Priest
Encampment)

Okanagan Brigade Trail

Summerland

Naramata

Naramata Creek

•(Shingle Creek Ranch)

Penticton

Area of
Wild Horse Canyon
in the Okanagan Valley,
British Columbia,
with both modern and historical landmarks.
The highlighted permanent syilx village
was only one of several such dwelling sites
in the area covered by the map.

Legend

Extent of 2003 fire

Pre-1900 permanent syilx village
called sənx̌ʷaqʷaʔstən

┼┼┼┼ Kettle Valley Railway

••••• Trails
(Historical Names)

Scale

0   10   20 km

0   5   10 miles

N

*Contains information licensed under the
Open Government Licence – Canada.*

Glossary and Pronunciation Guide for Syilx Words

Note: *ṅsyilxcín*, the syilx language, is itself a protocol teaching what it means to be *sqilxʷ*, including the belief that all living things are equal. This book follows the syilx protocol of not capitalizing *ṅsyilxcín* words that might be capitalized in English. For pronunciation guidance, see "Colville-Okanagan Salish Alphabet Song" on YouTube.

en'owkin (n'awqən)
enn-ow-kin
process of getting to the root of an issue by establishing clarification, conflict resolution, and voluntary participation in a group setting; this process fosters the idea of establishing the best solutions through respectful dialogue—creating consensus

nˇxaʔx̌ʔitkʷ
nn-ha-a-eet-koo
sacred spirit of the lake

sənx̌ʷaqʷaʔstən
sen-hwa-qwa-sten
place where arrowheads are shaped, referring to specific dwelling sites for thousands of people spread out along what is known today as Mission Creek in Kelowna, B.C.

sncəwips
sen-ch-wee-ps
phrase describing how the syilx/Okanagan people's collections,
including language, stories, and oral histories as well as three-dimensional and tangible objects, tell of their history and time on their lands; basically, a more inclusive way to refer to their heritage based on their perspectives as First Nations people

sqilxʷ
skay-lo-heh
a term meaning "the people"; a derivative of *stlsqilxʷ*, which refers to the original inhabitants of the syilx/Okanagan region

suʔwikst
soo-week-st
place where harsh weather, often including thunder and lightning, occurs (area in which Okanagan Mountain Provincial Park is located)

syilx
see-yeel-heh
used to describe the entire nation of *ṅsyilxcín*-speaking people,
incorporating the many districts and places in which they live; commonly understood as the action of weaving many strands to make one strong whole

sʔatqʷəɬp
s-at-qwa-el-hehl-p
ponderosa pine tree

xʷátik̇
hwa-teek
syilx place name for what is commonly known as Wild Horse Canyon, referring to the path that goes alongside or parallel to the lake there

ʔuknaqín
ook-na-kane
one of the districts within the entire syilx nation, specifically referring to the *sqilxʷ* who inhabit the territory known as the Okanagan Valley; also refers to carrying items, stories, and/or messages to the top or highest end

1780

Observing centuries-old traditions, a young Okanagan man follows an elk trail through a large, steep-walled canyon. He knows the area from watching a deer hunt last fall. Today, he is alone. The young man is on a quest to communicate with the four-legged animals, the birds, the water creatures, and the plants that live here. Seeking direction from them and the land, he waits without eating. He won't leave the canyon until he receives a message.

As the young man watches and listens near a tall yellow pine, coyotes pace the rim of the canyon. A red-winged blackbird high in the tree pecks at a pine cone. A seed falls, glances off the man's arm, and lands on a rock. Later, a garter snake slithers onto the rock to sun itself, nudging the seed to the ground. It comes to rest by jagged bark flakes shed by the pine.

Before the young man returns home to share his message with his elders, he uses the red-ochre and bear-grease paint he brought with him to record what he has learned. He paints on the smooth granite wall across the canyon from the yellow pine. His painting—a pictograph—will stay bright and clear for centuries.

1782

Rain and hail are pelting down.

The Okanagan people swiftly paddle their dugout canoes on Okanagan Lake. They come ashore in a protected bay.

Wild horses gallop into the big canyon to find shelter. They gather in a dry spot under a rocky overhang.

After the spring storm is over, the mares and foals spread out, grazing on bunchgrass. The stallion circles them, guarding his herd.

In the middle of the canyon, near the trail, a yellow pine seedling stretches its spindly stem to the sky. It tunnels its taproot deep into the ground. Sunlight glints off the pine's wet needles. When a squirrel barks, *kuk-kuk-kuk,* one foal shies. He leaps right over the seedling.

The Okanagan people leave some wild tobacco on shore to give thanks for shelter. They also place some in the water as an offering for safe travels. Then the people push off in their dugout canoes to continue their journey.

1786

The yellow pine sapling in the canyon is now as tall as a man. A deer browses on its needles. Inching up the yellow pine's trunk is a caterpillar wanting to nibble the needles, too. Near the treetop, a blue grouse snatches a bundle of needles for building her nest.

The deer pricks its ears at a rumbling sound. The ground trembles. Wild horses thunder past the sheer rock wall in the canyon. They can run no farther. They are trapped by the Okanagan people.

The wild horses neigh, snort, and mill about. They will be tamed. The Okanagan people will ride them throughout the Okanagan Valley and use them to carry heavy loads.

1800

The tender inner bark of young yellow pine is one of many welcome springtime foods for the Okanagan people. In summer, they gather saskatoon berries and dig up mariposa lily bulbs south of the canyon. They fill the woven baskets strapped to their prized horses. A woman collects plants for medicine and yellow pine pitch for making her containers waterproof. The *sqilxʷ* thank the plants for giving them what they need to survive.

In the fall, Okanagan hunters beach their dugout canoes in a cove near the canyon to stalk bighorn sheep and elk. As they approach with quiet steps, an elk scratches his neck on the rough bark of the young yellow pine.

1811

Across Okanagan Lake from the canyon, an Okanagan village Chief greets two fur traders who were granted passage and arrive at his village by a small lake. David Stuart and Ovid Montigny are passing through, looking for any Okanagan hunters who might want to trade their furs or some of their hardy, well-trained horses to the fur company.

At first, the Okanagan people are cautious. Then they agree to provide horses, and they offer the fur traders a place to rest until they move on.

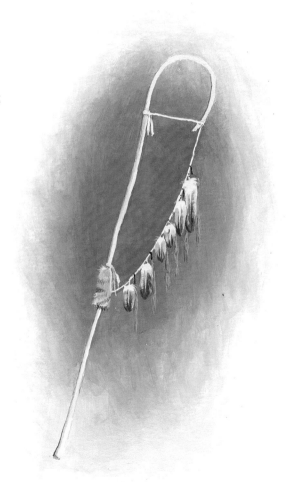

1830s

The explorer David Douglas gives the yellow pine species a new name—ponderosa pine. The ponderosa pine in the canyon now reaches as high as a five-storey building. A bald eagle takes off from its perch on an upper branch. Soaring to the west, the bird stares across Okanagan Lake at the dust billowing on the other side. Many horses in a long line are trekking south.

Powerful gusts of wind ruffle the eagle's feathers. The wind sweeps away the dust stirred up by the horses' hooves. Back in the canyon, the ponderosa pine sways and shakes. But the tree has a wide circle of roots that keeps it from blowing over in strong winds.

The horses carry furs and men in a fur brigade. In the lead is a rider wearing a tall black hat. He is the chief trader—the factor—of the fur traders. Horses without riders carry large, heavy packs instead. Wrapped tightly inside the leather covers are bales of fur from many northern animals. The packhorses walk in single file to form a pack train. Wranglers, mostly French-Canadians with some Okanagan men, handle several horses each.

The fur traders follow the Okanagan Brigade Trail. The route has brought them here to the Okanagan Valley all the way from Fort Kamloops. Now the trail will take them south to Fort Okanogan on the Columbia River.

A strong blast of wind breaks off small tree branches and they land on two packhorses. The animals squeal and rear. They bolt. Their fur bales wobble, then snag on low branches. Terrified, the horses break free. Leaving the bales behind, they gallop off. The wrangler rushes to secure his other horses. The two that escaped keep running. They will join a wild herd.

1858

Gold! The rush is on. Most gold-seekers travel through the Fraser Canyon, but a few follow the Okanagan Brigade Trail north to the goldfields. Some will find riches, but many will not. Everyone needs food and supplies. The first wagon train to reach the Okanagan Valley rumbles and pitches along the trail. But soon the trail gets too rugged and steep. The wagons must stop. How will the supplies reach the trading posts?

Joel Palmer, the leader, decides to unload the wagons and take them apart. The wagon-train workers chop down trees and build rafts. They move all of the supplies and wagon parts onto the rafts and float them a long way up Okanagan Lake and across to a creekside Okanagan village. The wagon train can continue its journey on the flat land.

What about the horses and oxen and cattle? The workers decide to herd the livestock south around the lake to the East Side Trail. They drive the animals toward the big canyon. Neighs, moos, and shouts fill the air. The noise is so loud, a mountain bluebird darts back to its nest hole high in a dead tree.

A wild stallion eyes the horses. He charges forward and steals a mare by herding her into the forest.

1859

A Catholic priest named Father Pandosy and a group of settlers ride into the Okanagan Valley from the south. At first an Okanagan leader, known to the Europeans as Chief White Hat, stops them. But then he directs them to the east side of Okanagan Lake, where they can keep travelling north. The group treks along the East Side Trail through the canyon to the Okanagan village by the creek. Father Pandosy establishes a settlement and a mission with a chapel and a school. He names the place L'Anse au Sable, or Sandy Cove. Children from ranches throughout the valley attend the school. The Okanagan people teach their children themselves and are hesitant to send any to the mission school but allow some to attend for a while.

One year, a wildfire races through the big canyon. Grasses, low bushes, and pine saplings burn, but the large ponderosa pine's thick bark protects it from the flames. A decade later, the ponderosa pine still has a black fire scar. White-headed woodpeckers and northern flickers cling to the tree's trunk. They peck at its bark and pull out insects that live inside.

The East Side Trail gets busier. Cattle and hog drivers herd animals to market through the canyon, now called Wild Horse Canyon. One day, a rattlesnake spooks a horse so badly it bucks off its rider. The cattle driver scrambles away from the snake to catch his horse before it can escape to join the wild horses.

1890s and 1907

More and more settlers move into the Okanagan Valley. The government enforces reserves where the Okanagan people are confined to live. Nobody asks for their input. Their traditional way of living has been taken away along with their high quality of life.

Sternwheeler ships sail up and down Okanagan Lake. They carry mail, passengers, groceries, and supplies. The winter of 1907 is so cold Okanagan Lake freezes over. The SS *Aberdeen* and the ice-breaking barge it is pushing get stuck, and ice-cutting saws have to be used to clear a path to Penticton.

A winter storm rips lower branches off the ponderosa pine in Wild Horse Canyon. The harsh wind forces wild horses to huddle underneath a rocky overhang to keep warm.

1910
to 1916

Work crews build the Kettle Valley Railway high in the mountains south of Wild Horse Canyon. Strong men cut down tall ponderosa pines and shape them into railway ties. When the railway is finished, trains will carry away ore and fruit and bring more settlers to the area.

The ponderosa pine in Wild Horse Canyon is now a little taller than a twelve-storey building. The tree could be made into many railway ties, but it is not close enough to the railway route to be cut down.

Far, far away, across the ocean to the east, the First World War is raging. The Canadian army needs more horses, so once again Okanagan riders are trapping wild horses. These horses will be tamed and sold to the army to be sent to Europe.

1926

Close to 20,000 horses are running free in British Columbia. Russia wants to buy as many wild horses as can be captured in the Okanagan Valley. It needs horses for its army and farms. Ranchers and cowboys—non-Indigenous and Okanagan—work hard to round up wild horses and bring them to the Brent family's Shingle Creek Ranch. The Russian army buys 1,400 of them. The cowboys and the Brent children herd these wild horses 23 kilometres to Penticton. At first they gallop to tire the horses and make them easier to control, and then they slow the pace. In the city, the animals are loaded into stock cars.

The wild horses are hauled by train to Vancouver and moved onto boats to sail to Russia.

In Wild Horse Canyon the cones of the ponderosa pine release seeds, which fall nearby. The seeds sprout and some grow into seedlings. But the many low-growing trees and bushes keep most seedlings from getting enough sunlight and water, so they do not survive.

1930s

Loggers cut down large trees in Wild Horse Canyon and use horses to haul away the logs. The ponderosa pine is 155 years old and so huge the loggers leave it in place.

Kelowna teenager Jim Browne builds corrals in Wild Horse Canyon. He rounds up horses to train and sell. Several years later, a bounty is set on wild horses because they are eating grass needed by ranchers' animals. Soon few wild horses are left in the Okanagan.

1944

One summer during the Second World War, Chinese-Canadian soldiers camp at a bay near Wild Horse Canyon where Okanagan hunters camped in the past. The soldiers are secretly being trained in commando skills like wilderness survival. In the canyon, they practise with explosives by blowing up an old empty cabin. Dunrobin's Bay, where they camped, gets renamed Commando Bay.

Wild Horse Canyon and a large part of the surrounding land become Okanagan Mountain Provincial Park. It is a wilderness park; the only way to visit is by boat, on foot, or by riding a mountain bike or a horse.

One year, Sheila Paynter, a local woman who loves hiking, walks all around Okanagan Lake. It's a hot day when she treks through Wild Horse Canyon. A slither of snakes appears—only garter, not rattlesnakes. She spots claw marks on a poplar tree, then a cougar's paw print on top of fresh elk tracks. She's thrilled to see a mountain goat stand on the rim of the canyon and stretch.

2003

Lightning strikes Squally Point on the western edge of Okanagan Mountain Provincial Park and sparks a wildfire. The firestorm roars through most of the park. The giant ponderosa pine has been growing in Wild Horse Canyon for 223 years. It is over 60 metres in height, as tall as a twenty-storey building. The old tree burns and is destroyed, along with most of the other mature trees in the park.

Seeds from many plants, including those used by the *sqilxʷ* for food and medicine, have been waiting for decades to sprout and now begin to grow. Small bushes and trees that shed their leaves in fall thrive in the park. They compete with tiny evergreens for sunlight and water. Conditions are drier today than they were years ago, but some evergreens have sprouted and are surviving. A seedling sheltered by the giant fallen tree in the canyon is a new ponderosa pine.

The firestorm cleared areas of the park, which then returned to rocky grassland. Bighorn sheep once lived in the park and can now live there again. Volunteers help government workers capture a small herd in the south Okanagan and bring them to Commando Bay near Wild Horse Canyon. An Okanagan man named Leon Louis prays, and the sheep are released. The animals explore their new home in the park.

The syilx people keep their language alive and celebrate the resurgence of their traditional way of life. In the Okanagan Valley south and west of Wild Horse Canyon, mostly on reserve land, several hundred wild horses survive and still roam free.

The History of
Wild Horse Canyon
and Area

Timeline

13,000 years ago	A kilometre-thick glacier covered the Okanagan Valley.
10,000 years ago to 300 years ago	Archaeological evidence is from 6,000 years ago, but some researchers believe the syilx people arrived in the Okanagan 10,000 years ago.
Well before the first explorers	The first horses arrived in the Okanagan Valley, and the Okanagan people developed into a horse-based culture.
1811	Fur traders were the first non-Indigenous persons on record to arrive in the Okanagan.
1812	Alexander Ross led a fur trading expedition through the Okanagan.
1824	Okanagan Brigade Trail was established from Fort Okanogan to Fort Kamloops.
1843 and 1845	The first Catholic priests arrived in the Okanagan Valley.
1847	The last fur brigade pack train travelled the Okanagan Brigade Trail.
1858 to 1860	The Fraser River Gold Rush was followed by the Cariboo Gold Rush and a minor rush at Rock Creek, south of Kelowna, B.C.
1858	Joel Palmer led the first wagon train to enter the Okanagan Valley.
1859	Father Pandosy and a group of settlers established a settlement and mission.
1860	Father Pandosy and assistants cleared the Mission Trail.
1865 to the 1890s	Cattle and hog drives occurred along the East Side Trail through Wild Horse Canyon.
Late 1800s	The federal government set up reserves for the Sylix people without consulting them.
1893, 1907, and 1914	SS *Aberdeen*, SS *Okanagan*, and SS *Sicamous*, steam-powered sternwheeler ships, launched on Okanagan Lake.
Early 1900s	First Nations reserve allotments were reduced by the provincial government.
1907	Okanagan Lake froze over, temporarily stranding a sternwheeler.
1910 to 1916	Kettle Valley Railway was built.

1914 to 1918	During the First World War, the Okanagan people supplied the Canadian army with green-broke (barely rideable) wild horses.
1924	The lake creature known as *nx̌aʔx̌ʔitkʷ* by the Okanagan people was named Ogopogo by non-Indigenous people.
1926	Russia bought wild horses from the Okanagan Valley.
1930s	Some people caught and sold wild horses from Wild Horse Canyon.
1939	Road building along the East Side Trail stopped near the canyon. Wild horses competed with ranchers' herds for rangeland. A bounty drastically reduced the number of wild horses.
1944	Chinese-Canadian soldiers trained in commando skills at Commando Bay and in Wild Horse Canyon.
1971	Horseback riders explored the entire original Hudson's Bay Company Brigade Trail.
1973	Okanagan Mountain Provincial Park was created.
2003	A lightning strike ignited the Okanagan Mountain Park firestorm.
2004 and onward	Forest and grassland regrow in Okanagan Mountain Provincial Park. Bighorn sheep have returned to the park, and some wild horses remain in the south Okanagan.

More about Wild Horse Canyon and Area

Syilx and Okanagan Territory and Wild Horse Canyon

This book is about one small part of the syilx traditional lands. The syilx people inhabit a large, unceded territory that extends from north of Revelstoke, British Columbia, in the north to Wilbur, Washington, in the south, and from the Nicola Valley in the west to the Kootenay Lakes in the east (see "Fur Brigade" map, p. 34). The syilx nation includes the *ʔuknaqínx*/Okanagan people (known as the Okanogan in the U.S.). Wild Horse Canyon is located within the Okanagan district. To learn more about the syilx people and the history and original meaning of the word *Okanagan*, see www.syilx.org and www.sncewips.com.

Before European settlers arrived in the Okanagan Valley, Wild Horse Canyon was known only as *xʷátik̓* in the syilx language, *ṅsyilxcín*. Non-Indigenous people began referring to the canyon as the Big Canyon, then Wild Horse Canyon because of free-ranging horses in the area.

Pictographs

Pictographs are located throughout B.C. They were created using ochre, a natural mineral pigment, combined with plants, roots, and animal fat. The Okanagan people used a variety of resources to create pigments that have lasted for thousands of years. Pictographs are recognized as the first form of written material in the Okanagan and are instructions that inform the people how to live in balance with the environment and with each other.

Yellow (Ponderosa) Pine

The yellow pine is called *sʔatqʷəłp* in the syilx language. The tree is sacred to syilx/Okanagan people in birth, life, and death; often yellow pine is used to mark graves. A new name for the yellow pine—*Pinus ponderosa* or ponderosa pine—was proposed by botanist-explorer David Douglas in 1827. He chose this name because of the tree's large size (*ponderosa* comes from the Latin for "weight," like *ponderous*). Ponderosa pine trees can grow to 70 metres in height and live on average 125 years, but some can live 500 years or even longer. To survive drought, ponderosa pines develop wide-reaching roots close to the surface to access dew and any rain that falls, and a deep central taproot to access water underground. A seedling's taproot grows deeper than the tiny tree is tall. The mature ponderosa pine's roots are widespread and keep the tree from blowing over in strong winds.

Trapping Wild Horses

The first horses arrived in the Okanagan well before the first explorers and were the descendants of European horses brought to Mexico by the conquistadors in the 1500s. Over time, some domesticated horses in the Okanagan Valley escaped to live wild.

The syilx people developed into a horse-based culture, at first using horses for transporting people and supplies, such as woven baskets full of berries, and for riding in battles. Later, horses were used in farming and cattle ranching, and in sporting events, such as rodeos and racing. Wild Horse Canyon was one location used by the Okanagan people as a wild horse trap.

Some syilx people measured their wealth by the number of horses their family owned: on average twelve, but some owned several hundred. Overall wealth and economy were based on the health of the surrounding environment. If the land, resources, and water were healthy and all of the people were being taken care of, then the community was recognized as wealthy. While recognizing the idea of wealth and having possessions, syilx people considered the greatest wealth to be knowing how to use resources in the most respectful manner.

A group of syilx people standing under a rack of drying fish, Enderby, B.C. (early 1900s). COURTESY KELOWNA PUBLIC ARCHIVES, KPA#7966

Living in Balance with the Environment

For thousands of years, the Okanagan people travelled to the Wild Horse Canyon area on foot or horseback, or in dugout canoes made from large black cottonwood trees. Before setting out on a journey, they would make an offering for safe travels. They came to hunt animals such as elk or bighorn sheep with bow and arrow. They used in-depth knowledge acquired through practice, experience, and ceremony when digging for medicinal plants and roots or gathering parts of the yellow pine as medicine for the skin or to be consumed for certain internal problems. Knowledge about when, where, why, and how to harvest in the most sustainable manner continues to be passed down from generation to generation. Plant foods included saskatoon berries, yellow pine seeds, potato-like mariposa lily bulbs, wild celery, bitterroot, and in spring the inner bark or cambium of young yellow pine. Yellow pine pitch was used to seal and waterproof containers. Syilx people carefully, with reverence, looked after the land, water, trees, berry bushes, fish, birds, and animals. They spoke to the plants as equals, thanking them, taking only what they needed, and never letting anything go to waste.

The language and laws of the syilx people were given to them thousands of years ago. Specific to the Okanagan people was knowledge of *nx̌aʔx̌ʔitkʷ*—"sacred spirit of the lake"—with its home in a cave beneath Squally Point, near Wild Horse Canyon. In 1924, non-Indigenous people began calling *nx̌aʔx̌ʔitkʷ* by the name Ogopogo, changing its identity from sacred spirit to lake monster.

1811—First Contact

The first recorded mention of non-Indigenous persons travelling through the Okanagan Valley is the account of a journey made by David Stuart and Ovid Montigny in the fall of 1811. The men travelled along the west side of Okanagan Lake with saddle and packhorses to set up the trade in furs between the First Nations and the Pacific Fur Company. The trails they followed were already in use by syilx people who travelled regularly through the entire unceded territory of the syilx Nation.

In 1812, Alexander Ross headed an expedition through the Okanagan Valley to set up a fur trading post at Fort Kamloops in the British Columbia Interior.

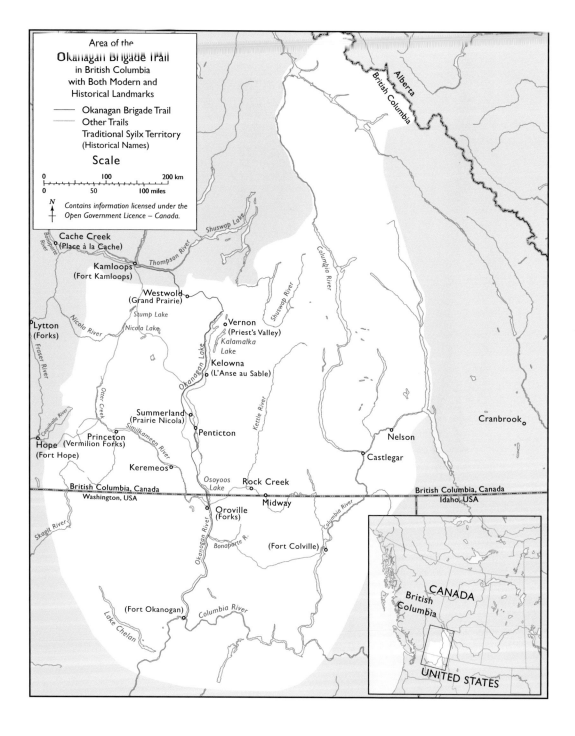

Area of the
Okanagan Brigade Trail
in British Columbia
with Both Modern and
Historical Landmarks

.... Okanagan Brigade Trail
.... Other Trails
Traditional Syilx Territory
(Historical Names)

Scale

0   100   200 km
0   50   100 miles

N
Contains information licensed under the
Open Government Licence – Canada.

1826 to 1847—Fur Brigade

In 1824, Tom McKay adapted pre-existing trails into the Okanagan Brigade Trail, part of the Hudson's Bay Company Brigade Trail, from Fort Okanogan (in current Washington State) to Fort Kamloops. The route travelled over a mountain pass and along the upper benches above Okanagan Lake, avoiding rivers and their floodplains. Stopping points were about every 30 kilometres—a day's travel—where the 100 to 125 horses could find grass to eat and water to drink, and the fur traders could set up camp. In spring, the brigade carried bales of furs south from New Caledonia in northern B.C. to Fort Okanogan on their way to London, England. In late summer, the brigade returned with supplies for the forts. The trail was in use from 1826 until the last pack train in 1847.

Some packhorses escaped and joined wild horse herds. The Okanagan people traded furs and horses to the fur companies in exchange for pots, pans, rifles, and clothing. French-Canadian and occasionally Okanagan riders worked as wranglers on the pack trains. Fur traders communicated with First Nations people using Chinook Jargon, which contained words from Nuu-chah-nulth, English, Chinook, French, Spanish, and Asian languages.

The fur trade brought many traders and settlers to the area and radically altered the traditional practices of the Okanagan people. Protocols that had been in place for thousands of years were discarded. Animal populations that once provided a high quality of life for the Okanagan people were destroyed or decimated. The Okanagan people began trapping and hunting for trade rather than sustenance. Assimilation took hold, and the people, lands, and resources were forever changed.

In 1971, horseback riders participated in a ride to follow the original Hudson's Bay Company Brigade Trail. Summerland, B.C., now has two parks to protect portions of the Okanagan Brigade Trail: the Priest Encampment at Priest Camp Historic Park and the Okanagan Fur Brigade Linear Park.

1858—Gold Rush and First Wagon Train

Gold was discovered on the Thompson River, near the Fraser River, in B.C. in 1858, beginning the Fraser River Gold Rush. By 1860, this rush was mostly over, but other gold rushes soon began: a major one to the Cariboo region and a minor one to Rock Creek, south of Kelowna.

The gold rush era was devastating in the Okanagan Valley. It drastically altered rivers, creeks, and fish populations, which wreaked havoc on the Okanagan people's way of being. The gold rush brought more people into the area who were not respectful of traditional Okanagan protocols, laws, and ways of living in balance with the environment. It encouraged the seeking of gold by any means necessary, including eliminating First Nation populations who resisted the newcomers and the destruction of lands that had not been legally transferred to the settlers. The devastation continues to affect syilx people today.

Joel Palmer, an American, led the first wagon train into the Okanagan Valley in 1858, having set out from Oregon. Out of the expedition's nine wagons full of supplies for trading posts to the north, two were damaged and left behind before reaching the valley. At Priest Encampment by Garnett Lake (now Garnet Lake, north of Summerland), the wagons could go no farther on the rugged trail. The problem was solved by bringing the wagons downhill to Okanagan Lake, taking them apart, and loading them and the supplies onto fifty rafts built using trees cut down beside the lake. The rafts were floated about 25 kilometres up the lake to the mouth of the creek near the permanent Okanagan village called *sənx̌ʷaqʷaʔstən*, in what is now Kelowna. The wagon train reformed to continue the journey north. Meanwhile, horses, oxen, and cattle were herded south back to Penticton, east around the foot of the lake, then north over the East Side Trail through Wild Horse Canyon to *sənx̌ʷaqʷaʔstən*. The East Side Trail was the original settling trail into the Okanagan Valley and used by syilx people for thousands of years. As it ran along the mountainside, it was too difficult for wagons.

1859—Father Pandosy

In October 1859, Cyprien Laurence and his wife, Teresa, joined Father Charles Pandosy and a party of

Roman Catholic missionaries and settlers to travel north from Colville (now in Washington State) to settle in the centre of the Okanagan Valley. In the south Okanagan (now Penticton), they were met by a large number of Okanagan people, including Chief White Hat and Chief *Sẁkʷńcut*/Sookinchute (from what is now Kelowna and West Kelowna). When Teresa's uncle, Chief White Hat, challenged Father Pandosy's party, Teresa spoke well of Father Pandosy, saying that he wanted to improve the lives of the Okanagan people. She convinced the Chief to spare the men's lives, for if he didn't, he would have to look after his niece for the rest of her life. Chief White Hat directed the group to continue their journey north, using the East Side Trail through Wild Horse Canyon on their way to *sənx̌ʷaqʷaʔstən*. The village Chief allowed Father Pandosy to live in the area, but not all Okanagan people were in favour of the idea. So Chief Sookinchute kept an eye on Father Pandosy for a while. It was good that he did, for without help and food from the Okanagan people, Father Pandosy would not have survived his first winter.

Later, Father Pandosy saw the need to replace the rugged East Side Trail. In 1860, *sqilx̌ʷ* and settlers worked together to build a new, smoother, and shorter trail over the mountain near Chute Lake and down to present-day Naramata. This trail was called the Upper Trail or Mission Trail.

Father Pandosy established a mission near *sənx̌ʷaqʷaʔstən* in a place he called L'Anse au Sable. He set up a chapel and a school. The children of about thirty ranch families from all over the south Okanagan attended. During the school terms, the children lived with ranchers near the mission. The school, where instruction was given in French, was open to Okanagan students, but the Okanagan people had well-established educational practices and were hesitant to allow their children to be taught by Father Pandosy. However, some Okanagan children attended the school for a short time.

Late 1800s—Cattle and Hog Drives

When raising cattle and hogs became the main industry in the Okanagan Valley, ranchers used the East Side Trail to move their livestock. Bunchgrass along the trail provided feed for the animals, and the cattle and hogs had easier footing through the canyon than along the Mission Trail. Ranchers asked for improvements to the East Side Trail and received government funds to have it re-blazed. The colonial influence placed a higher value on cattle than on horses, which had been valued by the Okanagan people for a long time. But raising cattle is hard on the environment.

In the extremely dry climate, lightning strikes could touch off wildfires, fed by dead trees, needles, and undergrowth. To lessen the risk of the whole forest being destroyed, and for other reasons such as improving berry and medicinal plant crops, the Okanagan people had traditionally cleared areas with regular controlled burns. This practice, however, was prohibited by the government in the late 1800s. Older ponderosa pines, which could withstand many fires thanks to their thick bark, now became vulnerable to more intense wildfires. As well, their seedlings struggled to survive in the overgrown forest.

Late 1800s to Early 1900s—Reserves, Sternwheelers, and Ice

At first the Okanagan people got along well with the settlers who occupied more and more land in the Okanagan Valley. But from the late 1800s on, the Okanagan people were required to live on reserves

Crowds at the CPR wharf greeting the SS *Okanagan* sternwheeler, Kelowna, B.C. (1909). COURTESY KELOWNA PUBLIC ARCHIVES, KPA#3111

set up by the government, even though they had not agreed to sell, trade, or give away any of their land. The reserve lands were not large enough for the Okanagan people to continue traditional practices, nor were they of good enough quality to grow crops. Legal restrictions on size of farmland and sales of crops grown on reserves, made it hard for the Okanagan people to participate in the development of the Okanagan Valley. The provincial government reduced the insufficient reserve lands even further in the early 1900s.

Between 1893 and 1914, the Canadian Pacific Railway launched three steam-powered sternwheeler ships on Okanagan Lake: the SS *Aberdeen*, SS *Okanagan*, and SS *Sicamous*. When Okanagan Lake froze over in 1907, even though the SS *Aberdeen* was using a barge in front to push through the ice, it was not able to reach Penticton. Citizens of that city, along with the ship's crew and passengers, used ice saws to cut a channel through the ice for the vessels to get to the wharf. The lake also froze over completely in January 1893, 1899, 1909, 1928, 1949, and 1950, and December 1968.

1910 to 1916—Kettle Valley Railway

The Kettle Valley Railway, from Midway, B.C., west to Hope, was part of the Canadian Pacific Railway. While building the railway, workers struggled under difficult working conditions, living in primitive camps of tents or log cabins. Loggers used broadaxes, crosscut saws, and portable mills to produce railway ties from ponderosa pine. Most of the route was finished when the railway opened in 1915, with the final section completed by 1916. Trains took ore from mines in the Kootenay area of B.C. and fruit from the Okanagan to faraway markets. Only a small portion of the railway near Summerland is still in use, now as a heritage railway. Much of the remaining railbed with its trestle bridges has been turned into a recreational trail that is part of the Trans Canada Trail.

During the First World War (1914–1918), the Okanagan people occasionally rounded up wild horses to supply the Canadian army with green-broke horses. These horses would allow a rider on their back but had minimal training.

Syilx cowboy dressed in his woollen chaps (ca. 1920–1939). COURTESY KELOWNA PUBLIC ARCHIVES, KPA#1629

1926—Wild Horses to Russia

Russian buyers wanted as many wild horses as possible, and ranchers in the Okanagan were eager to be rid of the animals. With close to 20,000 wild horses roaming free in B.C., ranchers had a hard time finding enough grazing range to feed their own horses and cattle. Ranchers and cowboys from all over the Okanagan set out to round up the wild horses. They herded the large number of horses to the Brent family's Shingle Creek Ranch (now called Bobtail Ranch) west of Penticton. After the Russian

Wild horse captured by Clarence and Sonny Favell in Wild Horse Canyon, about to be mounted by Sonny, with reins held by Cecil (called Bud or Buddy) Favell, both Clarence's sons (1930s). COURTESY JOAN MCCLELLAND

soldiers picked out the 1,400 horses they would buy for fifteen dollars each, the animals were branded on the hoof and tagged on the mane. Any horses not purchased were to be set free back where they had been rounded up. The Brent children joined the cowboys for the dangerous 23-kilometre ride to Penticton. The line of horses stretched for over 3 kilometres, creating a thunderous noise and giant clouds of dust. In Penticton, the horses were loaded into train stock cars and hauled to Vancouver to be loaded on boats to sail across the Pacific Ocean to Russia.

1930s—Horse Loggers and Catching Wild Horses

Logging of large, knot-free ponderosa pine took place in Wild Horse Canyon during the 1930s. Workhorses hauled the logs out of the canyon. Ponderosa pine was used in construction and to make boxes to ship fruit, and it is now used mainly for building doors, window frames, and furniture.

Some people earned money by catching wild horses in Wild Horse Canyon, then breaking and selling them. Three men from Kelowna who caught horses were teenager Jim Browne, who began in 1931, and Clarence and Sonny Favell, who were active during the 1930s and early 1940s. In 1939, a bounty was set on B.C.'s wild horses and within a few years most were caught. During the 1950s, a captured wild horse could be sold

for twenty dollars. In 2000, remains of a wooden corral topped by wire fencing reaching 3 metres above the ground could still be seen in the canyon.

1944—Commando Bay

Originally, Commando Bay was a safe harbour and campsite for the Okanagan people as they travelled by dugout canoe to the area to carry out traditional practices.

The Second World War lasted from 1939 to 1945. At Commando Bay and Wild Horse Canyon in 1944, Chinese-Canadian soldiers secretly trained for guerilla warfare in the South Pacific region. During their four months of training, they practised radio communication and ways to sabotage the enemy, including blowing up buildings. The young commandos successfully used their training behind enemy lines in Borneo. A bronze plaque at Commando Bay honours these soldiers and their contribution to Canada's war effort.

Plaque at Commando Bay dedicated to the Chinese-Canadian soldiers who trained in commando skills at that location during the Second World War. KAREN AUTIO PHOTO

1973—Okanagan Mountain Provincial Park

Okanagan Mountain Provincial Park is a Class A wilderness park of 11,038 hectares, established in 1973. The Class A designation means that the only development allowed is that which is required to maintain recreational use of the park. People continue to enjoy picnics on the beaches and hikes to see wild animals and scenic views. There are also hikes to small mountain lakes where visitors can fish for rainbow trout. The *ṅsyilxcín* name for this area is *suʔwikst*, "where harsh weather, often including thunder and lightning, occurs."

In 1989, Sheila Paynter, a naturalist, hiker, author, and matriarch of the pioneer Paynter family of Westbank, walked aound Okanagan Lake, a distance of 270 kilometres that took her twenty-four days to complete.

2003—Okanagan Mountain Park Firestorm

With fire suppression, the amount of natural fuel on the ground in Okanagan Mountain Provincial Park had grown significantly. The intense, lightning-sparked wildfire in 2003 destroyed most of the park's closed forest (thick with undergrowth and dead trees), leaving only small patches unburned. The firestorm also burned some areas of south Kelowna, including 239 homes, as well as several Kettle Valley Railway trestles. Insects, such as the mountain pine beetle, infested a number of the remaining living trees, causing further damage to the ecosystem. A provincial review of the impact of the firestorm recommended more controlled burning. Now the practice is being used in B.C. to better manage lands and forests.

2004 Onward—Rebirth

Although the park was now drier than it had been before the firestorm, the rebirth of the ponderosa pines slowly began. Mushrooms and grasses flourished, along with rodents that fed on the grass. Predators, such as coyotes and eagles, also increased in number. By 2010, redstem ceanothus bushes had started to grow in Okanagan Mountain Provincial Park—the heat from the firestorm had opened seeds that had been waiting to sprout for over a century. The park had fewer birds that live in closed forests (such as ruffed grouse, mountain chickadees,

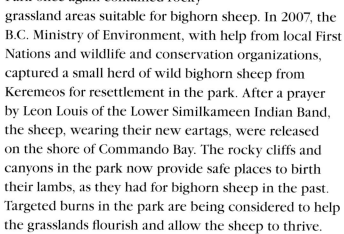

and red-breasted nuthatches) and a higher number of mountain bluebirds and olive-sided flycatchers than before the wildfire.

After the wildfire in 2003, Okanagan Mountain Provincial Park once again contained rocky grassland areas suitable for bighorn sheep. In 2007, the B.C. Ministry of Environment, with help from local First Nations and wildlife and conservation organizations, captured a small herd of wild bighorn sheep from Keremeos for resettlement in the park. After a prayer by Leon Louis of the Lower Similkameen Indian Band, the sheep, wearing their new eartags, were released on the shore of Commando Bay. The rocky cliffs and canyons in the park now provide safe places to birth their lambs, as they had for bighorn sheep in the past. Targeted burns in the park are being considered to help the grasslands flourish and allow the sheep to thrive.

The Okanagan educate their young people in *ṅsyilxcín*, the syilx language, and traditional customs to continue instilling pride in their heritage. The En'owkin Centre in Penticton and the Sncəwips Heritage Museum in West Kelowna play an important educational and supportive role regarding Indigenous culture, practice, and teachings. First Nations community schools also teach language and culture.

At least 600 wild horses still roam the south Okanagan, including reserve land near Penticton and Oliver, south and west of Wild Horse Canyon.

Index

Acknowledgements

Thank you to Christina Neale for introducing us to Jordan Coble, Westbank First Nation member and Cultural and Operations Administrator at the Sncəwips Heritage Museum. We are grateful beyond measure to Jordan, our advising editor, who reviewed the manuscript and illustrations for syilx historical and cultural accuracy, sharing knowledge and his love for the Okanagan. Thank you also to the Okanagan Nation Alliance for permission to use their territory map and wording to indicate the syilx traditional lands.

Kathryn Shoemaker graciously answered our many picture-book and illustration questions. The Okanagan Historical Society Reports provided a wealth of information; Sheila Paynter reviewed and added to the parts of the story about her walk around Okanagan Lake; Raf De Guevara took us by boat to Commando Bay so we could hike to Wild Horse Canyon; and David Gregory provided photographs of pictographs, did the historical review, and gave us a tour of the Okanagan Fur Brigade Trail. For their help with tracking down historical details of Kelowna, trail routes, Wild Horse Canyon, the Fur Brigade, Kettle Valley Railway, and/or commandoes' clothing, we are most grateful to Barbara Bell, Keith Boehmer, Jamie Browne, Jim Failes, Bob Hayes, Tara Hurley, Ken Mather, Peter Ord, Joe Smuin, Duane Thomson, and Maurice Williams. George Benmore guided us on our hikes from the end of Lakeshore Road into Wild Horse Canyon, and he shared his vast knowledge of Okanagan Mountain Provincial Park and his photo collection from regular hikes to the canyon.

Sincere thanks to Patricia Fraser, Eileen Holland, and Mary Ann Thompson for their valuable critiques of the manuscript. We count it a blessing to share life with you writerly women. What a joy and privilege to work with the incredible Sono Nis Press team: Diane Morriss, Laura Peetoom, Dawn Loewen, Frances Hunter, and Audrey McClellan. Thank you, Diane, for all you did to make this book a treasure and for connecting us with the talented and innovative Melanie Jeffs, publisher at Crwth Press, who brought this book to publication.

Loraine thanks Sherry Hamilton, secretary of Sənsisyustən School, and former principal Wayne Peterson for providing models for illustrations. Loraine enjoyed working with students Kaylynn Sandy, Xaydan Peterson, Wade Werstuik, and Cedarus Isaac Baker. When Loraine needed models for horseback riding illustrations, Fiona Griffiths of Trapalanda Farms provided pupils and horses for the action shots. Fiona's patient and enthusiastic pupils were Talia Wood, Shelanne Comfort, and Matthew Dobbs. And many thanks to Julia Bowers, the skilled photographer who captured the galloping riders in her amazing photographs. For other photographs of horses as models, Loraine thanks Jasmine Wood of Kelowna, B.C.; Lisa Martin-Gerdes of Redbud Ranch in California; Glenn Stewart of The Horse Ranch in B.C.; Elaine Christopher of Rocknhorse Acres in B.C.; Julie Tamisiea in North Carolina; Christine Mallon Hansen of Mallon Farm in Montana; Terri-Lynn Hughes of Fairly Big Farm in Goodwood, Ontario; Poppy Psyllakis of Victoria, B.C.; and photographers John T. Humphrey and Mary Cioffi working for Pine Nut Wild Horse Advocates in Nevada.

Karen's passion for historical details was invaluable to Loraine all through the process and helped immensely to create believable and accurate renderings. Loraine's wonderful husband, John, took over many home duties for two years to help her keep on schedule. When Loraine needed additional models for anything from loggers to cowboys, John and their sons, David and Andrew, faithfully came to her aid.

Karen thanks from the bottom of her heart her husband, Will—her constant encourager and support, and enthusiastic first audience of her work. Karen is immensely thankful to her illustrator, Loraine, whose eagle author eyes and lifelong experience with horses and living in the Okanagan meant she spotted bits in the text that needed changing. Loraine's determination ensured the historical details were as accurate as possible in her beautiful illustrations that bring the text and the history alive.

About the Author

KAREN AUTIO has long been intrigued by Wild Horse Canyon. The tales of syilx/Okanagan people trapping wild horses there piqued her interest. She started researching the history of the canyon and got hooked on exploring what had happened in the area over the past few centuries. When Karen imagined a ponderosa pine growing in the canyon for more than two centuries, this book began to take shape.

To learn more about Karen's other books for young readers, visit www.karenautio.com.

About the Illustrator

LORAINE KEMP has loved being an artist since she was barely old enough to hold a pencil. Living in the Okanagan Valley all her life and excelling at painting people and animals, especially horses, have given Loraine an edge for creating realistic renderings of her beloved home environment and its inhabitants.

To learn more about Loraine's artwork and writing, visit www.lorainekemp.com.